Praise for *The Intangibles*

"Enchanting . . . These poems suggest people should enjoy the fun of language while it lasts."

—*Publishers Weekly*

"Always count on Elaine Equi's nimble gymnastics to flip the ordinary around and create something rich and strange . . . These poems do not wear their brooding hearts on their sleeves but rather flirt and banter, drawing us close before revealing their ruminative complexities."

—Albert Mobilio, *Hyperallergic*

"This is a book for now and for the future, a panacea and antidote to the fear of the inane unknown. Equi's elegant control of line, image, percolating observation is always a taut surprise. I feel better already. Inside these subtle poems, complete little universes, there's never a dull moment."

—Anne Waldman, author of *Bard, Kinetic*

"If Emily Dickinson were alive today, her name would be Elaine Equi. Each of these poem gems is a secret; to know them, simply read them."

—Bob Holman, author of *The Unspoken*

"Mystery, romance, wisdom, whimsy, beatitude — this is what we crave in poetry and Elaine Equi delivers. In the divided camps of American poetry, she has forged an original style. Her persona stretches between past eras and coming frontiers. Formal structures are complemented by informal tones as she toggles from elegant to broad."

—Jeffrey Cyphers Wright, *American Book Review*

Praise for *Sentences and Rain*

"Equi relishes the stark, overlooked beauty of the quotidian in her curious, winding, fanciful [thirteenth] collection."

—*Publishers Weekly*

"[Equi is] genuinely funny—like all genuine humorists, she has depth, she picks targets, she's patient, she takes aim. . . . Equi gives us several drawing boards' worth of characters, or friendly caricatures, framed in a wry, almost lighthearted nostalgia."

—Stephanie Burt, *American Poets*

"If you can imagine it, you can probably find it here in one of Equi's lists of objects both real and surreal."

—Library Journal

"If there is a secret joy informing Equi's poetry, it is in the way she accepts the world as it is, without quarrel and without illusions except those that are sanctioned by art. Like a still-life specialist she gets you to see not only the red flesh of the watermelon but the beauty of the black seeds on it."

—Best American Poetry

Praise for *Click and Clone*

"Whether celebrating clones or revising Led Zeppelin ('That stairway only leads half-way to heaven'), Equi melds verse with aphorism, wisdom with wicked playfulness."

—Entertainment Weekly

"In an age of instant and infinite communication marked by blips, beeps, and tweets, [Equi] continues to streamline her unique vision. . . . This troubling topic, seemingly alien to a poetic sensibility, is indicative of Equi's reach into the future. She also keeps the past magically alive."

—The Brooklyn Rail

"Equi's newest collection is punchy and fast paced; saturated with an urban tang. Modern yet staunchly accessible in their quirkiness, her poems feel alive."

—Publishers Weekly

"Elaine Equi is not a poet's poet and not a people's poet, and yet she is both. Her poetry is wry and sparse. Often less than a page, her poems read something like eloquent one-liners that along with laughter effortlessly provoke profundity: a little Wang Wei, a little Frank O'Hara, a little Nicanor Parra, but mostly, just a little."

—Jesse Tangen-Mills, *Guernica*

Praise for *Ripple Effect*

Finalist for the L.A. Times Book Award
Shortlisted for the Griffin Poetry Prize

"Equi is a poet of transformations, exploring the pathway linking inner and outer worlds, dream life and lived life, heart and mind."

—Floyd Skloot, *The New York Times Book Review*

"Deft, delicate, subversive, and more quotable than any American poet who comes to mind."

—August Kleinzahler, author of *Snow Approaching on the Hudson*

"For thirty years Elaine Equi's alchemical poems have made dark magic from kitsch, from the burnt-out dead ends of the late twentieth and early twenty-first centuries. *Ripple Effect* brings them together in a way that makes us look with increased vigilance at the totems of our culture."

—Rae Armantrout, author of *Finalists*

"Elaine Equi's narrow lines are like the rungs of a ladder that one ascends while one is descending them. It's a motion like that in Wang Wei's lines, 'Stars / float up / toward dawn,' which she quotes in her cento, 'Wang Wei's Moon.' Or, as she beautifully puts it, 'Discreetly a breeze enters the room.'"

—John Ashbery, author of *Planisphere*

Praise for Elaine Equi

"These poems, brief as they sometimes are, simply-stated as they almost always are, open up a ground, a web, of the conscious and subconscious dailiness we all experience but rarely self-examine or seek to understand."

—*New York Journal of Books*

"There is a lot of fake poetry out there. Equi is real. She changes the way you look at things. You cannot fake the authenticity that informs even the most casual of her observations."

—David Lehman, series editor for *The Best American Poetry*

OUT OF THE BLANK

OTHER COFFEE HOUSE BOOKS BY ELAINE EQUI

The Intangibles, 2019
Sentences and Rain, 2015
Click and Clone, 2011
Ripple Effect: New & Selected Poems, 2007
The Cloud of Knowable Things, 2003
Voice-Over, 1998
Decoy, 1994
Surface Tension, 1989

OUT of the BLANK

Poems by Elaine Equi

COFFEE HOUSE PRESS MINNEAPOLIS · 2025

Cover design by Dirk Rowntree
Book design by Abbie Phelps

Coffee House Press books are available to the trade through our primary distributor, Consortium Book Sales & Distribution, cbsd.com or (800) 283-3572. For personal orders, catalogs, or other information, write to info@coffeehousepress.org.

Coffee House Press is a nonprofit literary publishing house. Support from private foundations, corporate giving programs, government programs, and generous individuals helps make the publication of our books possible. We gratefully acknowledge their support in detail in the back of this book.

LIBRARY OF CONGRESS CATALOGING-IN-PUBLICATION DATA

Names: Equi, Elaine, author.
Title: Out of the blank : poems / by Elaine Equi.
Description: Minneapolis : Coffee House Press, 2025.
Identifiers: LCCN 2024025344 (print) | LCCN 2024025345 (ebook) | ISBN 9781566897174 (paperback) | ISBN 9781566897181 (epub)
Subjects: LCGFT: Poetry.
Classification: LCC PS3555.Q5 O98 2025 (print) | LCC PS3555.Q5 (ebook) | DDC 811/.54—dc23/eng/20250617
LC record available at https://lccn.loc.gov/2024025344
LC ebook record available at https://lccn.loc.gov/2024025345

Thanks to the editors of the following magazines where some of these poems first appeared: *Action, Spectacle; Allium;* the *American Poetry Review; Big Other;* the *Brooklyn Rail; Columbia Poetry Review; Conjunctions; Court Green; Grand Journal; Hanging Loose; Julebord; KGB Bar Lit; Marsh Hawk Review; Mississippi Review; Plume; Posit; Three Fold.*

"Avoidance" was included in *The Best American Poetry 2024,* edited by Mary Jo Salter and David Lehman.

PRINTED IN THE UNITED STATES OF AMERICA

32 31 30 29 28 27 26 25 1 2 3 4 5 6 7 8

For my mother, Felicia, and my grandmother, Amina

TABLE OF CONTENTS

"Drawing a blank
permits one to sleep for a minute or so
nodding away and waking to find
on the island a shell with a sound."

BARBARA GUEST

"Own the blankness."

JOHN ASHBERY

OUT OF THE BLANK

JANUARY

Greetings from the first darkness,

prima materia,

moon enclosed in cloud caverns —
trailing a watery shadow, wet flame.

Winter, the brittle season,
further exfoliates the trees;

in the park glazes statues
with dirty rain.

It is not difficult for them
to hold a pose for centuries.

But what are you still thinking?
Is it better to forget it — or persevere?

I remember the statue of Goethe,
a not-so-jolly giant in Chicago,

and the one of Gandhi in New York,
striding through Union Square.

Once I actually saw someone snatch
the necklace of pink carnations

that had been draped like pom-poms
around his neck. It didn't faze him a bit.

Implacable, he just kept putting one foot,
always the same one, in front of the other.

THE MARROW

Of a poem.

Meat of meaning

that travels with Bashō
the narrow road –

network of veins
leading to leaf-lip.

Magnetic pull
of green-blooded words.

OUT OF THE BLANK

We waited for Word to arrive
like a messiah in a stagecoach
or a sheriff riding a thundercloud.
But she came without a name,
a sheer barely-there-ness,
teaching us first to hum
the song of the game show.
Essentially, nothing changed,
only now it seemed more colorful
and easily divided into categories — more fun.
Suddenly everyone took up a hobby.
Mine is getting in touch with
my antediluvian self — my inner reptile.
Fire and tools are still a long way off.
And language — well, who's to say
we haven't been speaking it all along.

SEERS

Eyes are like dice. They see by chance.

Of course, if they're healthy
they see what's in front of them —
what's given. But not all of it.

Certain saints and disturbed individuals
see what's not there —
have visions and hallucinations.

Some people only have eyes
for what they're looking for,
while others never find it,
even when it's staring right at them.

All these things can be true, but I think
eyes are like dice. They see by chance.

YELLOW LADDER

A yellow ladder
leans against
a redbrick wall
under a blue sky.

Beautiful.

But it doesn't lead
to a window,

and it's not tall enough
so someone could climb
over the wall.

Maybe a construction
worker left it there
temporarily.

But I don't think
a builder put it there.

It must have been an artist.

Nevertheless,
don't walk under it.

BUYING TIME

Is time always transparent –
the unwet water we live in like bacteria?

It should come in different shades;
be frosted and opaque.

Perhaps if it were something we bought,
like any other commodity,
there'd be more choices.

Many people, myself included,
feel there's not enough of it.

But I don't want it so I can do more.

I want it so I can do less
but take longer to do it.

A lot longer. And a lot less.

I want to find enlightenment
during happy hour
on a side street lit with neon rain.

Take little sips, with long naps in between.

TAKING STOCK

There I was —
mindfully minding
my own business.

Industriously
scanning every item
in my body

and sorting them
into bins of seeing,
hearing, feeling, thinking.

Hearing,
feeling,
feeling,
thinking,
hearing.

Labeling every thought
leaves little time to think them,
which is probably for the best.

Labeling every pain or sensation
can sometimes make them disappear.
Perhaps they were in your mind after all,
whatever that means.

I wonder what will become of me
and my ambition.

Not living — but labeling.

Not lost in thought —
just thinking, thinking.

EMOTIONS: A BOXED SET

Heebie-Jeebies

It's the kind of tail-in-socket anxiety
that plugs directly into the body —
manifesting in myriad symptoms of dis-ease.

Heat, chills, itch,
lightheadedness attached
to a lead weight.

A tilted feeling.
An agitated remix
of all of the above.

The scalp
(or is it the brain?)
aflame, like a burning bush.

Clarity

Being able to breathe.
In. Out.

The billowing curtain
of cilia and nerve endings
stirred by an oxygen breeze.

How long can I keep this up?
What could be better?

Appetite

Even when I'm not thinking about food,
I'm thinking about food.

I'm feeling the pulsations,

the vibrations of phantom food
calling.

The word “chicken”
becomes a mantra.

Burgers appear
like bloody daggers in *Macbeth.*

It seems fitting in old age
to return to an oral stage
when food was of
primary importance
and time was structured
around meals.

When you looked
at every object and wondered —
edible or not.

"I SAW DELIGHT"

I walked straight into the day's diamond mine

stuffing my eyes with as much dazzle
as would fit in the back pockets of my brain
and the dingy tote bag of my body.

The shadows were dark and luxurious
beneath silver trestles of light.

I saw a woman carrying the trophy of a gold balloon,
letting it bounce lightly above her head —
her thoughts golden.

Someone else was walking a diamond dog.
Each of its hairs was polished to perfection.

From every object, prisms of paths opened.

Where did they all lead?

Why would anyone want to be anyplace but here?

THE IRONIC SHIRT

Elegant yet
irreverent,

it bestows
a sort of saunter
on the wearer

like a white rum
and soda,

which is called
a Straw Hat.

THE WOUNDED CLOCK

Time is a
slow close-up

while waiting
for a wound
to close up

but once it heals,
everything
speeds up

and returns to
the surface again.

THE LONELY PARADE

Each
carries
their
parcels
of
sadness

through
the
twilight
village

under
the
illusion
they're
alone

when
really
they're
in
the
majority.

MY MOTHER AND I SEND EACH OTHER CIRCLES

Of light.

We telepathically juggle globes of color —
enclose ourselves in the space-capsule of their spheres.

I say:
Where are you?

She says:
I'm on the couch looking at the plant.
I'm on the couch looking at the TV.
I'm on the couch sprawled out with my feet on the cocktail table.
I'm in the kitchen looking across.
I'm in the bedroom lying down.
Where are you?

I say:
I'm in the chair looking at the door.
I'm standing up looking at the bookcase.
I'm in the bedroom, lying down.
I'm sitting on the bed looking at the wall.

Then one of us says:
What color would you like? You choose.

I'll take all gold.
I'll take pure white.
How about white with gold sprinkles?

I want green — all different shades.

What if we try a rainbow for today?

Okay, stay right there.
I'm sending it now.

I’m still sending it.

It’s sent.

I DON'T WISH TO BE A VAMPIRE

With centuries of memory
stored in a youthful body.

It is — or could be — such a pleasure
if we didn't fear it so much,

to get old and indulge in
subversive acts of dawdling,

withering, forgetting with impunity,
letting go of ambition served too long,

its bittersweet ligatures finally breaking
down and dissolving.

While others feverishly train
body and brain in gyms,

let me cultivate the corpse flower,
listen to it like a radio in a small room

quietly playing its hypnotic
melodic overture of decomposition.

IDLE CHATTER

Please, distract me
for another minute or two,

another hour.

Distract me for
several more years —

they're yours.

Keep me from
my true purpose

unless that purpose
be to pursue distraction

like a scholar or a monk
who shuns all else.

SLOW CHALK

I believe in the angel of
if not progress,
then process.

I pray to the air
that carries words away
to an outer being
made of possibility.

I believe in the resemblance
of unrelated things
uniting them as family
beyond blood.

In the university
of the universe
all books are holy
as light   and night

and the livestock of languages
penned within.

UNCOLLECTED

My poem with the blank stare and secret smirk.

My poem with the mojo of a thousand emojis.

My poem like a tame ocean.

My anorexic poem sucking for days on a single syllable.

My hearty Midwestern potluck poem.

My poem with the heady air of an Alpine inn.

My poem that still suffers in the twenty-first century from neurasthenia.

My city poem with its chorus of paper-skyscraper dolls.

My lace-edged unromanticism.

My poem that likes talking to strangers.

My pathetic poem.

My homeopathic poem.

My glow-in-the-dark poem.

My poem that is finished by elves.

EASTER MONDAY

It was Easter yesterday,
but news travels slow,

and some are still fighting
the same old war.

All day I keep hoping
to run into myself

on corners that almost
but never quite meet.

Rain tinsels taxis.
Like sleepwalkers,

buildings rise from puddles
waving their blurry bricks.

GNOSTIC TUESDAY

They live among us.

The Incognito —

those who know
but do not tell.

*

I said, "The weather is nice today."

To which he replied,
with a shrug indicating the trees,
cars, sunshine,

as if across the street
were another world,

"I don't care anything
about what goes on out there."

CRAYON

Weather colors the day.

Breath inflates our aches.

Bobbing along the surface.

Why must I always
finish my sentences?

It's as if
          and now can't stop.

GOBLET

my grape my globe my gape

my glazed my glare my grimace

my glint my grant my giant

my goose my gravy my grail

RECURRING DOG

In the first dream, the dog is disguised as a cat.

In the second dream, when I pet him, the dog turns into chocolate.

In the third dream, the dog is a ball of dirty yarn that I scoop up and lay over my chest to muffle the sound of my rapidly beating heart.

Recently, I was surprised to discover that the idea of "care animals" has caught on even in the dream world. Apparently, these nocturnal service animals have been trained by totem leaders in the collective unconscious, to gently nuzzle sleepers who show signs — tossing, turning, twitching, grinding — of experiencing particularly gruesome or humiliating nightmares. But they do it with sweetness and finesse, so the person isn't forced to wake abruptly — instead is gradually led on an invisible leash to explore more pleasant terrains before morning.

BLANK BAG

I dream of losing
my purse again.

Have gone out
without my personhood.

Am just a penniless
ghost again,

unable to buy
a return ticket.

The sales counter
is the border
of this country.

BUILDING A WALL

With dreamless bricks
embedded in darkness.

This construction has
been going on for weeks.

I wake up tired,

not good-tired
like the twelve princesses
who wear out their shoes
every night at the disco,

more like the guy
in "The Cask of Amontillado."

Which one?
The guy inside the wall
or the one who put him there?

Both.

THREE KITCHENS

Nestle inside each other
like Russian dolls.

First comes the pantry
where the child learns
to read the calendar
and practices stirring
with ladles and spoons.

Next is the family kitchen
where the family seldom gathers.
It is like the concession stand
of a nearly empty movie theater
late in the afternoon.

Third is the restaurant's loud kitchen
of many hands banging pots and pans,
where the angry chef curses the potatoes
and curses the customers,
and the dishwasher, like a dragon,
exhales clouds of steam.

Three different kitchens,

three different hungers
eating together —

chewing slowly —

each one swallowed
by the next.

MAPLE

Leave me alone with a jug of this syrup and who knows what maple mayhem I'll get into.

Once someone asked me for my favorite word. I wanted to say "malice" but that sounded too mean, so I gave them "maple."

It did the trick — totally threw them off the scent of my aggression.

But I honestly do love maple, with its high-pitched sweetness, so piercing only a dog can hear it.

The taste speaks to some darkness deep in my soul where a sleepwalker stands bathed in the light of an open refrigerator, swigging the sticky liquid, like bourbon, straight from the bottle.

"I am drinking the blood," she chants. "I am drinking the blood of the forest."

TOPOGRAPHY

We are congealed in them.

Hats, phones, gestures buried
deep in the billowing mountains.

Once she was a small boy.

Then he became an old woman
stirring the pot.

"For a long time now I haven't been I."

Sometimes, the only reason
she gets out of bed is to decide
which fragrance — which pronoun — to wear.

We all contain multitudes.

There is work to be undone.

LEE

When the teacher asked the girl if there was a nickname she'd like to be called, some voice in her spoke right up and said, "Lee," which was strange because no one had ever called her Lee. In her whole life, she had never known a Lee except for Sara Lee, the famous baker whose cheesecake her mother sometimes served to company. So when the teacher said, "Alright then, Lee," she had to train herself to respond and look as if she really were this Lee character. Lee, she was sure, was a guy who rode horses – a cowboy-loner type. There was something sullen, almost tragic about him as if he knew he was not long for this world. The name never stuck, and by next year she was telling everyone to call her Amber.

THE RED NOTEBOOK

The Simple Explanation

I must remind
myself

I am not losing
my mind,

I just need
a haircut.

Tragic Sweater

In the moths
that followed

the ________

she found
herself slowly
unraveling.

Team Players

Jekyll and Hyde
Martin and Lewis
Lewis and Clark

Lap of Luxury

Why not curl up
on the velvet couch
in the loudly
purring room?

Minimalist Critique

Just because it's short doesn't mean it's good.
But it usually is.

Today's Affirmation

I've got a new leash on life.

SEVEN-WORD SELFIES

1.

Stripend

Antiquarium

Stormative

Umbiblical

Prismantic

Slimmetry

Orphantom

2.

Oblonging

Tendecency

Roaricle

Bellchemy

Histoic

Serenada

Noctournament

A CHANT IN THE MANNER OF ROBERT LAX

1.

Arise
Arise
Arise

Repose
Repose
Repose

Arise
Arise
Arise

Repose
Repose
Repose

Arise
Arise
Arise

Repose
Repose
Repose

Arise
Arise
Arise

Repose
Repose
Repose

Arise

Arise
Arise

Repose
Repose
Repose

2.

arise	repose
arise	repose
repose	arise
repose	arise
repose	arise
repose	arise
arise	repose
arise	repose

MID-SEPTEMBER

Closing the windows.
Turning on the AC.

Opening the windows.
Turning off the air.

Turning on the fan.
Changing into shorts.

Closing the windows again
and turning on the air.

Leaving the AC on in one room
but not the other.

Leaving the AC on and windows
open at the same time.

Wasteful — yes — but also
refreshing.

Striving to find the perfect balance
between inside and out,

golden ratio of summer to fall.

WITHOUT SCHOOL, THERE IS NO AUTUMN

Cider press of hours
spent procrastinating.

Slow ripening of books.

A fact emerges: the date when
some long-forgotten war began.

The name of a soldier grazes the ear
like a kiss evaporating.

How do we learn?
How dare we learn?

School is a kind of bondage —
a corset made of cruel repetition.

Once all knowledge was forbidden.

But now even trees realize they're naked.

MISTAKES

I said the wrong thing.

I said the right thing in the wrong way.

I waited too long to say the right thing. By then it was the wrong time,
so I said nothing.

I said the right thing but didn't mean it.

I thought the right thing but couldn't believe it.

I bought the wrong book.

I tried to read the right book but found it dull,
and never finished.

I wrote the wrong book.

It took years, but I'd like to exchange it for a new one.

FLOATERS

Dark globes
bubble up.

Bright scarabs
scuttle by.

You try to close
your fist around them

but can't — find
they've vanished

only to reappear
elsewhere, like stray

musical notes
detached from a score

or ink spots
leaving muddy tracks

splashed across
the transom

between observer
and observed.

WHAT DID I DO WITH MY *KING LEAR*?

I saw it.
It's here.

I even took it
down off the shelf
and said,
"Here's *King Lear*."

Then I put it back.

There used to be
two of him.

We got rid of one.

But the other is here
somewhere.

Ah, there's *King Lear*!

Where was he?

He was sitting
right next to
Ezra Pound's
Guide to Kulchur.

WISPS O' WILL

A Tedious Brief
My Bland Husband
Like Knitters in the Sun
Green and Yellow Melancholy

Slubber the Gloss
With a Greedy Ear
Taste Your Legs
Drink the Air

Delaying, Not Forgetting
Old Fond Paradoxes
Demi-puppets
Sleepy Language

Wiselier
Furtherer
Bewhored
Beshrewed

O Notable Strumpet
Why Stare You So?

WEATHER VANE

If only I had one,
I'd keep it for a pet.

Let it perch on the roof
tethered to the wind,

warbling a tinny,
whirring song.

Let the body of the house
sag beneath its talons,

go limp as it lifts
it and us up — up.

Gilded bird,
crowing at midnight,

pecking at the grain
of stars.

MUSICAL CALENDAR

January
is jazzy, cool, existential,
beat, black-and-white
snow showers of notes.

February
carries its torch songs
sung by Billie, and Julie,
and Judy, and Edith.

March
is not straightforward,
is not a march.
It sends mixed messages—
Aaron Copland's optimism
muddled with Bernard Herrmann's
dark obsessive throb.

April
is an aria sung
by Kermit the Frog.

May
is acid house rave.

June
was made for moonwalking
and surf punk weddings
on the beach.

July
is a blue dream
trance lullaby.

August
is an anthem
big enough
to swell a stadium
with bloodlust
and pride.

"*September*
Song" is a classic
written in 1938
by Kurt Weill &
Maxwell Anderson.

October
is demon-driven thrash metal
or a fey goth girl group
singing folk horror tunes.

November
is a big country song
with cowboy chorus
and pumpkin pie.

December
From Tchaikovsky
to the Ventures,
from Bing Crosby to
Christmas on Death Row,
there's always room
for another holiday album.

LORCA'S GUITAR

I saw it on display,
the case lined with red velvet,

like part of his body — his voice —
or a companion of his voice

laid out in an open casket
sealed within a glass box.

It was a small instrument,
almost a ukulele,

this skiff that carried him
across the lake of deep song.

I stood before it, listened,
and heard nothing.

No "wind in the olive trees,
wind in the mountains."

I thought it looked homesick, as the poet
himself had been homesick in New York.

I hope there is a museum guard,
some shy boy,

who comes when no one is around
and plays it.

THAT FEELING

of waking up
and feeling

I could go
anywhere,

not that I
had to go,

but that it
was there.

I want to
remember that.

3/18/20

NONSPECIFIC ELEGY

This is not
just about
keeping busy.

I miss you.

Even if we
never spoke,

or were only
briefly underground,

overhearing
each other's music,

breathing shared air
together –

the loss is profound.

Walking down
an empty avenue
in spring,

I miss you.

A PARENTHESIS OF BELLS

Bleating between
morning and evening,

bleeding a pastel
pastoral memory

into the urban
gridlock of
lockdown days.

Spring with its
forsythia basket

only heightens
the sense of loss.

Yes, it's true;
once we were
shepherds,

sipping a latte
on our way
to the bank.

THE ETERNITY SHOW

Mind that the children who carry
the sacred chafing dish take care
not to scorch their paper wings.

Led by the Mauve One, a slow
procession marks the graduation
of one world to the next.

Hell is when you have to keep going
from screen to frozen screen.
Heaven is when you're already there

in your favorite loungewear
and can watch everyone else
play the fool card or have to go fish.

Tonight, let's rewrite the old tragic myths
so they end with chicken and waffles in front of
the TV — lazy paddleboats going up the River Styx.

EVERYONE INTO THE PYRAMID

Grab your pets and your iPads,

your altars, your avatars,
and alter egos.

I drink the last light.

I am the hours that fly.

Take your sex toys and your almonds
dusted with pink Himalayan salt.

Don't forget the Book of Passwords.

Everyone into the pyramid now.

INDOOR WEATHER

Outside, there is no shortage of weather.

A symphony of seasons plays 24/7.

But indoor weather is more like chamber music.

A leaky cloud drips from the ceiling
into the wooden pail of Chopin's piano.

Certain homesick individuals bring commemorative weather
like a spicy wind from a distant land to circulate among
their belongings and soothe them.

Some examples of indoor weather from film
would be the hallucinatory electrical storm
that chases the reporter feigning insanity
down the asylum hall in Sam Fuller's *Shock Corridor.*

Or those inexplicable demon-infested cold spots
that love to haunt abodes from Amityville to Hill House.

At the end of *Citizen Kane,* once the snow globe
of memory breaks, flurries fill the room
swirling around Orson Welles's massive head.

No use for his old sled in Xanadu.

MOVEMENTS

Ascending

Lazily –

like smoke
through air.

Threading the Keyhole

The art of staring at a door
until it opens.

Really more a process
of visualizing what's
on the other side –

the way hunters
are said to identify
with their prey.

The 360

A circling motion
made with the mind
or a camera

or by physically
walking around
a chosen object

in order to view it
from a number
of vantage points.

Perhaps also a way

of capturing it in
an invisible net.

Very French.

In a Minor Key

Pensive.

Subdued.

Hesitant.

Halting.

Slowed by ambivalence.

But still, inching forward.

TWO POSTCARDS FROM ANCA

1.

A bouquet
of fuzzy stems,

limbs going
every which way.

Droopy
            lemonhead

hung
            over

blue glass
ocean
            bowl

like an anchor.

2.

A bundle of
abundance.

Pink vertical
twigs branch

above smaller
red stick figure,

earth angel,

corn-husk priestess

who tends
the unlit
candle's well.

ON A CAROUSEL

Pineapple and
blues for breakfast.

Sweet orange tea
in the afternoon.

Winter light's
wounded brightness.

I am thinking of
Jared Leto's hair.

MUSE

I miss
the airs

we used
to walk on,

the word-holes
we'd sneak
through.

Perhaps you don't
recognize me

sitting here
watching
The Voice.

SLEEPING WITH THE PAST

Pulling
          cloud
off
          of bone

like one of
the undead.

*

The TV is still on.

Its muffled voices,

sepia light
seeps
into everything.

IN MEMORIAM

I enjoy filling
the ice cube tray –

holding it
under the tap,
moving it
slightly left
or right

to insure each cube
is created
more or less
equally.

I know machines
could easily,
would gladly,
do it for me.

But I prefer
to do it manually –

tucking the tray
into the freezer,
anticipating tomorrow's
first cold drink.

The rattle of ice in a glass
is a happy sound

that reminds me of my father
fixing a triple-vodka martini.

Whenever we heard it,
we knew he was home.

INTERIORS

You can always recede further,
tunnel deeper.

Darkness is relative
where backlit screens abound.

Today everyone is inside
the cold.

We say, “What are you watching?”

We’re bingeing a show about
a living doll that replaces a dead child.

They’re bingeing a show about
vampires and witches.

All afternoon, the episodes
accumulate like supernatural snow.

CALLING ALL CALIBANS

Melodious monsters
from the ugly depths
of their desperate desire
for delicate things.

But why would a beast
long for beauty?

Or money?

Heart —
a harpsicord

beneath powdered
platinum moonlight wig.

O THOU, MY

I will raise a psalm
like a palm tree to thee.

I am but a cog
in a song,

a tortoise
of no great purpose,

a tourist in
my own hometown.

Hurry to me
for I am thy servant.

O Lord, make no delay.

An army of shadows
seeks to devour my flesh.

Confound my predators,
and I will praise thee to infinity.

I will praise thee when rich.

I will praise thee in a ditch.

I will praise thee like a rock star
picking up a Grammy.

Anoint me with calm,

and I will raise a psalm
like a palm tree to thee
O my Lord.

SPIDER SOUP AND MAGIC ROCKS

I did it –

drained the shallow
bowl of sweet, sharp
spider's liqueur,

then pocketed
the magic rocks
from the scholar's library.

Stole his dusty memories,
replacing them with ordinary
stones from the yard.

Didn't hesitate.
Didn't stop to think.
Didn't think I had it in me.

But I did.

RAIN PICNIC

Eating
            seared
                        salmon

serenaded
            by
                rain.

It's refreshing to watch it pour
from our outdoor-seating
curbside shack,

really just a tin roof
extended over the table
like an umbrella.

The golden beets, the pickled cabbage —
everything tastes extra moist and delicious.

And it is, I must say, entertaining
to watch pedestrians hurry by
getting soaked.

Some stoic, others giddy.

Most caught unaware
since there was zero chance of precipitation
in today's forecast.

But it's really coming down,
so I order a second lemon-mint soda
allowing us to linger another fifteen minutes
before getting the check.

By then, the surprise shower has stopped

as suddenly as it began.

We should do this again more often.

REPLACEMENT PARTS

Riding in a taxi on a grey day.

It seems everything is under construction
behind a mesh veil of soot and scaffolds.

A new city is emerging so gradually
no one will notice, the way they say
a body replaces all its cells every seven years.

It will feel as if nothing has changed,
and yet none of this — not a bit of us —
will remain.

A different woman will be riding
in a different taxi on a cold but sunny day.

MY NAME IS SNOW

She wanted to meet someone in the coffee shop of the motel. I know because I *was* her, but when passed through the sieve of memory, I became someone looking for her. No one remembered having seen her. The coffee shop had closed years ago and was now a fancy restaurant serving brunch. I drove to different parts of the city. I visited a few monuments and took some photos. At last, I returned to the place where the coffee shop would have been — and there it was. Someone told me I had just missed her. She had been there waiting but had gone home. I went to her house and found her there, just as they'd said. "Who are you?" she asked. "My name is Snow," I said, and then I melted.

FLOWERS DON'T SPEAK TO ME ANYMORE

I've lost the habit

of arranging
        my life

                around them.

No longer wander
in search of
        papyrus
        or poppies,

lilacs or lilies,

though their perfume
still haunts me
from bottles, not vases.

It's less subtle,
a chemical synthesis,

but the thing I miss most
are their colors —

the language their colors
would speak around the house
when it was just us.

FLAMING STAR

Going to the movies
was anarchic back then.

You walked in on the story
wherever it was in the telling,

happy just to sit in the dark
and listen to these giants –
be with them for an hour or two.

Women often taking off
their clothes.

Men often shooting
or getting shot.

One of the first ones
I ever saw was *Flaming Star*.

I remember sad-eyed Elvis
staring out at us
as if we were a prairie.

AVOIDANCE

I'm not watching the movie –
just looking up from my book now and then,

puzzled by the actors whispering urgently
as if prompting each other to remember their lines.

If only they would recite the words on the page
in front of me, I'd be more attentive.

Actually, I see I'm doing more than simply
not watching; I am actively avoiding

the film like an unpleasant topic disguised
in furs and jewels. Something about it offends me.

I suppose I could put on a different movie,
but you were sleeping so peacefully,

I didn't want to risk waking you from the lullaby
of this pretentious dated melodrama.

Not only am I busy avoiding the movie,
I am using it as an excuse to avoid continuing

to read the book I had started, which to be honest
isn't so great either. It would seem any activity

one chooses might be motivated by the desire
to get away from something else.

So, I have even physically moved to a different
room. I can still hear the movie, but faintly,

as a kind of spoken music of emotional tones,
and without the visuals, it's almost enjoyable.

I’ve also put my book down and have begun
writing this poem — obviously the activity

I was avoiding all along, and now can pursue
wholeheartedly to the exclusion of everything else.

TIMING IS EVERYTHING

Hear and there
Know and then
Once in a wild
Knot yet

AUTOBIO' 69

Hatched
Crated
Carried

        Porch
        Parakeet

Nuns
        Torture
                Zine
                        Smoke

Scarlet   Spies
Courtly   Subterfuge

Chemical
Twins
Hitchhike

        Foppish
        Freshman
        Blues

*

Kismet
Puppet   Palace
Kitsch

Dayshift
        Workshop

Nightshift
        Restaurant

Beyond Baroque

*

Mulberry
Plumbs

Written Skyline

Lyric
Coffeehouse

Inn
One
Ear

Out
And About

Recording

*

Ambient Noise

Sleepless Analysis

Dizzy
Whirlpool
Adrift

Roof-deck Portal

Ashen Tower

Cloudy
Occluded
Collision

*

Retro
Reverb
Ripples

Activate Inner

Zero Hour
Cuckoo Clock

Curating
Colors And Airs

ÉDOUARD VUILLARD

I like the busy patterns
dotted with flowers,
shawls and lawns,
collars of Édouard Vuillard.

They make me think
of old women having a shot
of brandy in their tea.
O the pleasures of nightcaps,
bingo, and sachet.

It is nice to think of becoming
an old lady even if you
already are one. When you
take off your glasses,
a young girl stares out
at the fuzzy world, amazed
to have made it this far.

CALLIOPE AT NIGHT

What is that sound?

Is an ice cream truck idylling
at the end of the world?

Is that wobbly tune meant to lull
or lure me from my bed?

O Calliope — in a singing match
I am no match for you.

Do not turn me into a magpie
as you did the daughters of Pierus.

Mother of Orpheus — why did you run away
from the epic poem to join the circus?

Calliope, Calliope,
I can hear you calling me at night.

MY MOTHER DREAMS OF DYING

It was like a painting,
but real.

A landscape with buildings,
not high-rises.

Antique buildings,
but new.

And there was a fountain
and a mausoleum.

I saw women walking
in robes.

Not white robes like you think they wear in heaven,
just robes.

I had lost my cell phone
and I wanted to leave.

I saw a man
(he was wearing a robe too)

and asked him how I could get out of there.
He said, "You could leave if you really want to.

There are a lot of different doors."
Then I found myself lying on the ground

and all the energy was draining out of me.
It was beautiful.

PMA

I was in the basement
of a superstore
looking for a bathroom.

Walking for what
felt like miles
past nondescript aisles

and isles of boxes
stacked into fortresses.

Some shelves were empty,
some stocked with generic versions
of every conceivable thing.

I wasn't desperate or destitute,
judgmental or confused.

Instead, I had a pleasant, relaxed
"seek and you shall find" attitude.

IN A STRIPED LIGHT

Jerome looks up
from his book.

Like St. Jerome,
he is always
looking up
from his book.

The green lamp
behind him is on.

The green lamp
is always on.

Its lampshade looks
like a hat —
almost a fez —
levitating
above his head.

The late-afternoon
sun coming through
the mini blinds

causes his hair,
face, shirt, chair
to unfurl
in blue diagonals.

Like a flag,
even the window's
shadow flaps
against the wall.

“T” AS IN TAUT

for Tom Clark

To hold the line steady

through countless
poem-years.

Not a slacker,
he taught us that —

as one who truly
stands by his word

when words
seldom mean what
they’re meant to.

C. R.

Even if he didn't want to practice law,
Charles Reznikoff was a brilliant lawyer
in his poems.

Justice — or rather Injustice — was his muse.

We hear the testimony
of witness after witness.

But who or what is still on trial?

Perhaps we are — each of us.

He weighs our hearts
against the feather of truth.

RENDEZVOUS

Your poems were already
thinking these things
when I came into the world.

Words I would arrive at later —
elated.

There is a postcard in my book
to mark today's page.

It is a photo by Lartigue
of a woman in a restaurant,
her face hidden beneath
a wide-brimmed hat.

She is not looking at
the pale mountains
or the sea over her shoulder.

She is reading a book —
waiting for someone to join her.

YOUR LOVE HOROSCOPE

You fill the life you share with others with love and affliction.
Loved ones annoy any time they spend with you,
and appreciate you as a thoughtful and simulating lover.
Your unnatural approach makes you an attractive
and despicable partner to have — something you can use
to your advantage, especially if you find you're singular.

LIONS FOR LEOS

The lazy MGM lion watching old movies high in midsummer sky.

Bert Lahr's Cowardly Lion, his mane permed and perfumed into curls.

Stone lions guarding libraries and temples of art.

Corpse-and-Christian-eating lions' bad breath.

Leo, Leo, Leo — nickname of the Sun — short for Helios, Helios, Helios.

Marlon Brando as a blond SS officer in *The Young Lions*.

Peter O'Toole looking long in the tooth as *The Lion in Winter*.

The godlike voice of James Earl Jones in *The Lion King*.

Mick Jagger playing maracas in his Leo glyph T-shirt and flowing blood-red scarf.

Literary lions: fiery Shelley, majestic Ashbery, and the pet lions of poets praised in verse.

David Shapiro spending an afternoon with a lion in a villanelle.

Robert Duncan "harkening to the lion-smell of a poem."

Tom Raworth's lion, lion: "the book they found in the lion's lair."

Allen Ginsberg's lion for real with "implacable yellow eye in red halo of fur."

Michael McClure's rebel lions, "Ghhrarrr!"

FADED FLASHBACK

Fled
        Fragment

Fishy
        Franchise

Final
        Fluke

Fads
        Famines

Fizz
        Foam

Flail
        Fix

Feeling
        Feral

Fake
        Forgers

Famous
        Friends

NATURE ABHORS A VACUUM CLEANER

Verlaine is great, but I prefer Vallejo.

Vespers is a lovely time of day.

I would describe myself as vibrantly vague.

Being a vestal virgin is a vocation, not a career.

Vampires have always vacationed in Venice.

On the veranda, Vincent and Vivien sipped vermouth.

Under the viaduct, vagabonds smoked weed.

The Visigoths would certainly vandalize, but the Vandals were not Visigoths.

Bobby Vinton was known as the Polish Prince; Mel Tormé as the Velvet Fog.

Vicki is so vegan, she even feeds her Venus flytrap veggie burgers.

The verdict is in, vests are on the verge of making a big comeback.

Everybody strike a pose and vogue, vogue, vogue.

WASHINGTON SQUARE

Choosing the Hot Seat

Ignored the shade

in favor of
a sun-baked
stone bench.

Hours later,

the ass, still warm,
remembers.

Beware of

Shirtless
        skateboarders

cutting
        quick
                diagonals

like knives
        frosting
                invisible cake.

Tobacco Breeze

As if
the whole park

were smoking
a cigarette

and had
just exhaled.

NEVER HAVE I EVER

for David Trinidad

Never have I ever
seen such a pink sky

like the tonsils and gums
of a hippo

yawning as we ride
over the bridge

where a sugar factory
sweetens the river

and tall buildings melt
into the water.

THE CRAFT

Many people want to find magic,
like a new car or computer,
want to put magic to work
making more money or keeping
them young and immortal.
These are the same things
people have always wanted
which is how magic grew
into capitalism with magic symbols
printed on every dollar.
If only someone would find
a new use for this old technology —
would magic become magical again?

THE WITCHES' OPEN HOUSE

for Toni Simon

It is very airy –

has no walls,
no roof,
no door.

There are columns of stones
that rise like smoke

and stand precariously
but never fall.

These stones
(which may once have been birds)

are easy to animate
and rearrange to make
stone tables and stone chairs.

It is an energy field.
A cape of space.

Many may pass
and not know it's there.

HAVE IT YOUR WAY

moonlight
headlights

headlights
moonlight

moonlight
headlights

the crimson
(not golden)
arches of

Burger King
in the distance

SEASONAL

Finally,
summer.

Endless
summer
begins.

Finally, endless
begins.

Endless, endlessly

endless

summer
          summer
                    summer

fanning out
in all directions

finally ends.

NOTES

"I Saw Delight" is a one-line poem by Robert Creeley called "Homage to Hank Williams." It was published as a bumper sticker by the Alternative Press in Grindstone City, Michigan.

"My Mother and I Send Each Other Circles" is a ritual my mother, who is ninety-nine, and I perform as part of our daily phone conversation. Before hanging up, we visualize each other surrounded by a globe of colored light. It's similar to the way people on Facebook say "sending light," only we use different colors to suit our moods.

"Wisps o' Will" is a list of some of my favorite Shakespearean snippets.

"That Feeling" is the only dated poem in the collection. It seems relevant to know that it was written during the first few weeks of things closing due to the pandemic.

"Two Postcards from Anca" is an ekphrastic poem written from two images sent to me by my friend, Anca Cristofovici, a French novelist and scholar of photography, film, and literature.

"Autobio' 69" is a word list poem marking my sixty-ninth birthday. I thought it would be a fun minimalist exercise to only allow myself one word per year to tell my story.

"Lions for Leos" is a litany celebrating lions in film, poetry, and music. Coincidentally, Leo happens to be my zodiac sign.

Coffee House Press began as a small letterpress operation in 1972 and has grown into an internationally renowned nonprofit publisher of literary fiction, essay, poetry, and other work that doesn't fit neatly into genre categories.

Coffee House is both a publisher and an arts organization. Through our Books in Action program and publications, we've become interdisciplinary collaborators and incubators for new work and audience experiences. Our vision for the future is one where a publisher is a catalyst and connector.

LITERATURE
is not the same thing as
PUBLISHING

Funder Acknowledgments

Coffee House Press is an internationally renowned independent book publisher and arts nonprofit based in Minneapolis, MN; through its literary publications and *Books in Action* program, Coffee House acts as a catalyst and connector—between authors and readers, ideas and resources, creativity and community, inspiration and action.

Coffee House Press books are made possible through the generous support of grants and donations from corporations, state and federal grant programs, family foundations, and the many individuals who believe in the transformational power of literature. This activity is made possible by the voters of Minnesota through a Minnesota State Arts Board Operating Support grant, thanks to the legislative appropriation from the Arts and Cultural Heritage Fund. Coffee House also receives major operating support from the Amazon Literary Partnership, Jerome Foundation, Literary Arts Emergency Fund, McKnight Foundation, and the National Endowment for the Arts (NEA). To find out more about how NEA grants impact individuals and communities, visit www.arts.gov.

Coffee House Press receives additional support from Bookmobile; the Buckley Charitable Fund; Dorsey & Whitney LLP; the Gaea Foundation; the Schwab Charitable Fund; and the U.S. Bank Foundation.

The Publisher's Circle of Coffee House Press

Publisher's Circle members make significant contributions to Coffee House Press's annual giving campaign. Understanding that a strong financial base is necessary for the press to meet the challenges and opportunities that arise each year, this group plays a crucial part in the success of Coffee House's mission.

Recent Publisher's Circle members include many anonymous donors, Patricia A. Beithon, Theodore Cornwell, Jane Dalrymple-Hollo, Mary Ebert and Paul Stembler, Kamilah Foreman, Eva Galiber, Roger Hale and Nor Hall, William Hardacker, Randy Hartten and Ron Lotz, Carl and Heidi Horsch, Amy L. Hubbard and Geoffrey J. Kehoe Fund of the St. Paul & Minnesota Foundation, Hyde Family Charitable Fund, Kenneth & Susan Kahn, the Kenneth Koch Literary Estate, Cinda Kornblum, the Lenfestey Family Foundation, Carol and Aaron Mack, Gillian McCain, Mary and Malcolm McDermid, Daniel N. Smith III and Maureen Millea Smith, Vance Opperman, Mr. Pancks' Fund in memory of Graham Kimpton, Alan Polsky, Robin Preble, Ronald Restrepo and Candace S. Baggett, Steve Smith, Jeffrey Sugerman and Sarah Schultz, Paul Thissen, Grant Wood, Margaret Wurtele, Jeremy M. Davies, Robin Chemers Neustein, Dorsey and Whitney Foundation, The Buckley Charitable Fund, Elizabeth Schnieders, Allyson Tucker, and Aptara Inc.

For more information about the Publisher's Circle and other ways to support Coffee House Press books, authors, and activities, please visit www.coffeehousepress.org/pages/donate or contact us at info@coffeehousepress.org.

PHOTO © JEROME SALA

Elaine Equi was born in Oak Park, Illinois, in 1953. She is the author of many books of poetry, including *Voice-Over,* which was chosen by Thom Gunn for the 1999 San Francisco State Poetry Award; *Ripple Effect: New & Selected Poems,* which was a finalist for the Los Angeles Times Book Prize in Poetry and on the short list for the Griffin Poetry Prize; and *The Intangibles.* In 2023 she was the guest editor of the annual anthology *The Best American Poetry.*

Widely published and anthologized, her work is included in *The Norton Anthology of Postmodern American Poetry,* and several editions of *The Best American Poetry*. Over the years, her witty, aphoristic, and innovative work has become nationally and internationally known. Her poems have been translated into Italian, French, Spanish, Russian, Chinese, Croatian, and Arabic. She has taught in many creative writing programs, including those at New York University, City College of New York, and The New School. The recipient of a Guggenheim Fellowship, she lives in New York City with her husband, the poet Jerome Sala.

Out of the Blank was designed by Abbie Phelps.
Text is set in Source Serif Pro.